The Rise of Media

The Rise of Media

A Discussion of Communication Methods

Eugene Hertzberg

Writers Club Press
San Jose New York Lincoln Shanghai

The Rise of Media
A Discussion of Communication Methods

Writers Club Press
an imprint of iUniverse, Inc.

For information address:
iUniverse, Inc.
5220 S. 16th St., Suite 200
Lincoln, NE 68512
www.iuniverse.com

ISBN: 0-595-20547-X

Printed in the United States of America

Epigraph

I never think of the future—it comes soon enough.

—*Albert Einstein*

Contents

Preface

This writing is intended to provide a background into some of the past and present forms of media. This book represents three years of research.

Acknowledgements

To my parents, with love and gratitude.

Introduction

Marshall McLuhan believed that "the medium is the message." When a new medium is introduced it changes the way people think and provides a new way to perceive the world. In the early twentieth century radio was one of the main sources for news and entertainment. However, with the end of World War II came a booming economy where people had more money to spend freely. The emergence of the television industry in the 1940's brought a great social change to America and left a dramatic impact on the future of the radio industry. The rapid expansion of the Internet in the early 1990's provides first hand information on the development of a new medium. Internet access is becoming affordable for a majority and stands to challenge the future of television.

Chapter One

History

James Baughman writes in *The Republic of Mass Culture* that many Americans wanted to follow the events of World War II. The two major mediums were either the newspaper or the radio, with the radio being favored. The radio was "regarded primarily as cheap and convenient entertainment..." (Baughman 2). The radio had many advantages over the newspaper because it was live, and provided instant news updates. The radio also "...offered the voice of the president and his supporters and the unfiltered sensation of being there" (3). However people continued to read newspapers. Only now, "most Americans in 1945 who read in the evening had the radio on" (16). Radio had such a dominance that "by 1945 an American home or apartment was more likely to have a radio than indoor plumbing or a telephone" (16). The radio was popular and television was not yet in the thoughts of the mass media.

The mass media had "…found the war a stimulating diversion, for some a profitable one. Peace seemed only to promise better days" (Baughman 31). In 1947, following the end of World War II three of the major radio networks; NBC, CBS, and ABC made the first step into television by starting regularly scheduled broadcasts. The networks "…aired live dramas, and though some Hollywood performers participated, even these efforts at art could not be taken too seriously" (41). These first television programs were poorly done when compared with the movies of the time. Yet people were buying television sets in great numbers and "the percentage of homes with TV sets shot up from 0.4 percent in 1948 to 9.0 percent in 1950, 23.5 percent in 1951, and 34.2 percent in 1952" (42). Television replaced the radio rapidly because:

> Almost regardless of income, families with children were likely to secure a receiver. TV afforded cheaper entertainment for parents, who were spared the cost of hiring a babysitter in order to visit the local movie house. During the day, television kept youngsters

occupied, often in a separate 'family room,' and out of mischief. (42)

The television was so popular that "by 1956 just under two-thirds of all homes had one or more TV receivers" (42). It was now clear that television was an established medium because "magazines and newspapers no longer drew the eyes of so many readers" (58).

The television was following the radio in the sense that it was geared toward entertainment (Baughman 60). This was clear when "survey after survey indicated that a majority of TV users considered television a diversion...it had entertained them" (61). The predominance of the TV set had surpassed the radio: "By the late 1950's...visitors to the family den rarely spotted the once large radio receiver" (65). Statistically the evidence was even more compelling:

> Between 1948 and 1958, Americans who tradition-
> ally had listened to the network radio shows in the
> evening by the mid fifties watched network televi-
> sion programs. According to the A. C. Nielsen
> Company, the average American family's radio lis-
> tening per day dropped by 50 percent, from 4.4
> hours in 1948 to 2.2 hours in 1956. (65)

By the 1960's the use of television had increased even more to where "...92.6 percent of all households had at least one TV set; 22 percent had more than one" (91). The amount of time people spent watching television also rose from "…5.85 hours in 1963 to 6.50 hours in 1970" (91).

The 1960's had proven television's popularity as "…all but one of television's rivals had reconciled themselves to being secondary services" (Baughman 117). The other mediums now "…fought over that part of the consumer's time *not* devoted to television" (117). But radio was still popular because its role in people's daily lives had changed:

> Although radio remained a secondary mass cultural activity for most, the opportunities for listening increased over the decade.… The larger number of Americans who commuted to work by automobile were more likely to have car radios; indeed, for most a radio had come to be regarded as 'standard' rather than optional equipment. (130)

Radio had managed to survive, but as a secondary medium. More cars than ever had radios, with a sharp increase "…from 68.2 percent in 1960 to 92.5 percent in 1970" (130).

Radio had a firm grasp on the adolescent population and now mainly played music. Teenagers had a strong preference for the radio because: "…the typical teenager of the sixties preferred the company of peers and listening to a rock DJ on a local station to sitting with parents and younger siblings before the TV set" (Baughman 132). The radio provided top 40 songs, which exclusively appealed to the adolescent crowd. The radio had become a major source for music; it no longer concentrated on sitcoms. Music appealed to all ages of the population. However the television responded to the interests of the young viewer with programs like "Saturday Night Live," which in 1975 "appeared late in the evening, when most adults had gone to bed or had yet to return" (195). In 1981 the all music cable channel "MTV" started to show music videos.

Television was an instant success because it provided people with a new way to be entertained. As the TV industry continued to grow in the late 1970's and 1980's more specialized cable channels emerged. These channels provided people with content in one area, such as news or comedy. The television replaced the radio's central role in the household. However, it more importantly helped to redefine the secondary role of the radio; in cars and as a source for music. Although television was popular its viewers: "…typically finished watching a TV news program without remembering its major points" (Baughman 221). The television was "entertaining but not very informative" (221). Television had a weakness that could be exploited.

The development and rise of the Internet provides a major challenge to television. The Internet is a connection among computers (servers) that communicate with each other through standardized protocols. No central facility organizes communication; rather, each server is connected to a number of other servers, so connections between two servers are often routed through a number of different intermediate computers. Users of the Internet can connect their computer to these servers, usually via telephone service and modem; if they lack direct access to them (History of the Internet). The Internet includes Web sites, list-servs, newsgroups, and e-mail.

The Internet emerged during the 1960's as a project of the United States government's Department of Defense, to create a non-centralized network designed to survive partial outages (i.e. nuclear war) and still function when parts of the network were down or destroyed. This project was called ARPANET (Advanced Research Projects Agency Network), created by the Pentagon's Advanced Research Projects Agency established in 1969 to provide a secure and survivable communications network for organizations engaged in defense-related research (History of the Internet).

The Internet dramatically changed from its original intent and in 1985 became a source for "educational facilities, academic researchers, government agencies, and international research organizations" (History of the Internet). The use of the Internet expanded and by the 1990's the Internet experienced explosive growth. It is estimated that the number of computers connected to the Internet was doubling every year. By mid-1994 the Internet connected an estimated two million computers in more than 100 countries, serving some 23 million users. Many commercial computer network and data services also provided at least indirect connection to the Internet. It was also estimated that at this rapid growth everyone in the world would have an e-mail address by the year 2000 (History of the Internet).

The Internet provided a way for people to take better control of what they viewed through more specialized sites. The

Internet provides "[a] virtual frontier to expand our access to information and to increase our knowledge and understanding of public opinion, political behavior, social trends and lifestyles...cyberspace permits us to move beyond traditional face-to-face, mail and telephone..." (Fisher, Margolis, & Resnick, 11-12). A survey by The Pew Research Center in 1998 found that: "Increasingly people without college training...with modest incomes, and women are joining the ranks of Internet users." The Internet has become more widespread, while in 1996 only "23 percent of Americans were going online," in 1998 the number jumped to "41 percent of adults using the Internet" (The Pew Research Center, 1998).

The greatest impact of the Internet can be found at colleges and universities across the country because of the high-speed connections they have. A New York Times article states that "[u]se of the Internet as an educational tool by college freshman has become so prevalent as to be practically a way of life..." (Honan, 1999). A survey conducted in the fall of 1998 by the American Council on Education finds that "82.9 percent of new freshman – more than 4 out of 5 students – say they are using the Internet for research or homework. Nearly two-thirds, 65.9 percent report they communicate by e-mail" (American Council on Education).

A survey in 1999 by The Pew Research Center found that 30 percent of people ages 18 to 29 started using the Internet over one year ago. Twenty-five percent aged 18 to 29 started using the Internet within the past year. The survey also found that 52 percent of people aged 30 to 49 started using the

Internet in the past year. Thirty-nine percent of people who started using the Internet over a year ago use the Internet for pleasure. 52 percent of people who started using the Internet within the year also use the Internet mainly for pleasure. It appears that Internet access is also based on income. 45 percent of those surveyed earned more than fifty thousand dollars a year and had started using the Internet more than a year ago. Only 16 percent of those who earned fewer than thirty thousand dollars a year had started using the Internet more than a year ago.

Chapter Two

Specialization of Mass Media

The article *Power to the People (Meter)*, by Barnes and Thomson, describes the specialization of mass media. Magazines such as "Life" targeted a wide range of audiences, and as a result lost the attention of advertisers. This was due to a new trend on the part of advertisers to target a selected audience. Companies made products that were geared towards a specific group of the population, and no longer wanted to waste money on an uninterested population. Television provided a method for advertisers to gain more feed back on a targeted audience. This was due to the advent of new technologies, like the "Nelson Ratings," that could track who watched what. Barnes and Thomson's opinion on media specialization contrasts Ben Bagdikian's dominating view of media. However their view is supported by Jim Carroll's view that specialists can remain competitive.

Barnes and Thomson see the future of television as "...losing its grip on the masses" (75). This is because of a trend in advertisers to target specialized channels like "ESPN" over mass appeal channels like "USA Network." By focusing on a specific population, advertisers can better deliver their message. It is ratings that determine what people will watch and advertisers focus on ratings. Without advertisers the future of a television station is dismal.

Bagdikian, a prominent media critic, disagrees with the idea of specialization because of his documentation on trends. He is "...very concerned with the fact that as these media corporations get bigger and bigger and bigger, the tiny box called 'news' gets more and more obscure within the huge organization" (The Media Monopoly 2000). He sees many alarming facts such as the large number of television stations, magazines, and publishers. What is alarming is that out of the twenty-five thousand different media outlets, only twenty-three dominate. This decreasing number of dominant companies creates a decline in diversity and competition. This means that companies do not specialize, but instead try to monopolize. For example if a company like "Coca Cola" buys a publishing company, it will create negative political implications. Pressure from the ownership not to print certain stories would impact content.

Bagdikian believes that diversity is essential for democracy to survive. There must be a free flowing exchange of ideas and opinions. However this does not exist in instances where companies over step their bounds and buy into other industries. It is easy for big companies to do this because their costs are cheaper than smaller ones. And as the number of firms with ownership decreases, the quality goes down. Bagdikian sees the media industry as dominated by a few companies that have overstepped into other industries in order to cut costs, and have not been focusing on specializing.

Jim Carroll's opinion is more inline with that of Barnes and Thomson. Carroll is best known for his ability to communicate the value of technology and networks. He examined a large number of newspapers to track shifts in concentration. The shifts in concentration followed generalists versus specialists. The generalists were the papers that targeted a wide selection of the audience, like *The New York Times*. The specialists were papers geared towards a select audience, like *The Wall Street Journal* and *Creative Loafing*.

Carroll found that as concentration increased, the specialists thrived. This was due to the opening in terrain as the big generalist slugged it out. Carroll had found that the dominance of a few large firms did not reduce competition. This positive relationship allowed for specialists to survive. Carroll believes that the media industry is competitive, and that specialists can do well despite the small number of big firms.

Barnes and Thomson focus on specialization of companies in order to make money more efficiently. They qualify Bagdikian's argument by showing that specialization is really the key to the media industry. Barnes and Thomson disprove his ideas through their analysis of the advertising medium. They believe that advertising is the reason that diversity can exist. Advertisers target specific groups of people, and as a whole this creates a diversity. If all advertisers targeted the same population, there would be little difference across the media industry.

Barnes and Thomson believe advertising creates a competition for quality. With specialized audiences being the target, firms are looking for the best ways to reach them. In the instance of the television industry the demand for quality comes from reporting services like the "Nelson Ratings." Firms want more precise reports of who their products are reaching. And television stations want to sell their station as the best place for a firm to advertise. This contrasts Bagdikian's view on quality. He believes that quality decreases because a few firms dominate. He thinks this decrease in quality is also due the cost cutting policies of the few large firms.

Barnes and Thomson support Carroll's argument of specialization. Both attribute a competitive industry to the specialization. Barnes and Thomson believe that advertising plays a major role and do not focus on the big firms. Whereas

Carroll believes that specialists can survive because of big firms. They both are strong supporters of specialization as driving the media industry.

Chapter Three

Mass Culture Theorists

Mass culture theorists were concerned about the media industries and their pursuit of profit. They predicted that the noticeable rise, in expressive goods being sold for profit, would create more bad products. This "co-modification" would put price tags on items that were once priceless. They also predicted a transfer in production from individuals to corporations. This process would standardize content, leaving little marginal differentiation. Their belief was that once companies figured out what was successful, they would never stray from it. This would lead to a decrease in diversity, along with a decrease in innovation. Baker and Faulkner believed that the rise of the blockbuster created commercial pressures making revenue a main goal of movie firms. Litman and Ahn believed that several commercial factors can help and hurt a movies success.

Mass Culture Theorists had different opinions about the media firms and their markets. Some theorists believed that the firms could make you purchase things, while others thought that firms could find out what it was you would purchase. However they failed to overlook the difficulties that firms face in real life. One example can be seen in RCA's attempt to sell "Big Band" music to a public that was mostly interested in buying other types of music. RCA spent a lot of money on advertising with the belief that they could influence people to buy the music. However it was a complete failure. This proves that media firms cannot influence people to the extent at which some believe, no matter how powerful the firm.

Other Mass Culture Theorists believed in the importance of segmentation, specialization, and diversity. Firms used to target mass audiences, seeking to become more generalized. This was clearly seen in the early television industry, where the three main networks received the majority of the firms business. They believed that this limited diversity because of the limited number of options. However the Mass Culture Theorists didn't accurately account for segmentation and specialization because they were in a time where the big firms dominated. Eventually firms began to target segmented markets, with an emphasis on specialized channels. The Mass Culture Theorists were restricted by the time they were writing in. They could not foresee the wide range of products that are now available. They wrongly believed that diversity would only be harmed through the process of segmentation. However research proves that diversity goes up and down over time.

In the article *Role as Resource* Baker and Faulkner argue that the rise of the blockbuster created a commercial shift by film-makers to a combinatorial form. During the pre-blockbuster period films weren't viewed as major sources of revenue. However this began to change as the population expanded and discretionary dollars increased. This created a surge in the amount of money spent on films, pushing some of them over the million-dollar mark. The first signal of this change was seen with the great success of "The Godfather," in 1972, and "Jaws," in 1975. These two films proved that there was a growing audience for movies, and that the right elements could exploit this. With movies now grossing huge amounts, others sought to replicate their success. This created a surge of attempts to build on preexisting and proven models. For this many people tried to buy ideas from other areas of the media and convert them into movies. Others turned to established stars for clout, and to the theaters themselves for guarantees on their movie.

Baker and Faulkner are quick to point out that most attempts to replicate the blockbuster were unsuccessful. Yet with the firm establishment of the blockbuster the rules of the game had been dramatically changed. The specialized producer emerged as a result of the blockbuster. It became essential to concentrate on the "deal-making" aspect of the movies because of the increasing complexity and price of making a film. The specialized producer does not deal with the filmmaking itself, but rather the financial aspects of the movie. This meant that the producer now had to be able to attract investors and prove that the project was going to be a blockbuster. This redefinition and consolidation of roles also carried over to other areas of filmmaking, with an emphasis on those who had good track records or proven talent. This occurred because of the commercial pressures to reach the largest audience and make the most money.

In the article *"Predicting Financial Success of Motion Pictures"* Litman and Ahn report on the findings of research relating the success of a motion picture to several variables. They concluded that production costs, reviews, presence of superstars, the summer season, and G-rated pictures were positively related with the success of a movie. They focus on the commercial pressures on a movie when it is released. A movie is under intense pressure to do well when it is released. This directly influences the success of a movie in other areas such as when it goes to videotape, becomes a sequel, releases related paraphernalia, and experiences foreign success.

However Litman and Ahn say that the potential for a movie's success is limited by many of the same factors. One important factor is the reviews that a movie receives, which can have serious negative impacts. The number of screens on which a movie is released can also have serious limiting effects on a movie's success. Another limitation is a movie's foreign potential. Many movies seek to compensate for poor domestic sales through the foreign market. However the foreign market has been very unpredictable, and proves to be a challenge to domestic movies. In the case of "*Waterworld*" this proved beneficial. With poor domestic revenues, it made a profit through video sales and foreign release.

Chapter Four

Media Contents Effects

The Mass Culture Theorists overlooked the way media content affected people. There was a change in the focus of research on media content in the 1940's. People began studying the relationship of media content to the audience. Gamson and Modigliana brought out this change in their study on the depictions of nuclear power in *Media Discourse and Public Opinion on Nuclear Power*. They discussed the different stages of nuclear power, and how they were depicted.

From their article it became clear that media content should be treated as problematic because there are many ways to present even a straightforward issue. Media content does effect how people perceive the world because it sensitizes people.

Paul Lazarsfeld believed that the Mass Culture Theory wrongly followed the "magic bullet hypothesis." This was the belief that media content was fairly unambiguous in its meaning and that its impact on the audience is fairly uniform. He conducted a study of how and why people voted the way they did called "The Peoples' Choice." He concluded that the role of media content was relatively weak when compared to opinion leaders, people that gave solid advice. Yet when the media content was made accessible to these leaders they could then exert their influence on their peers. He also found that the opinion leaders only were interested in information that was consistent with their opinions. Lazarsfeld had a "minimal effect" view on the influence of media. From his study he concluded that media content's influence was weak when compared with people's advice and opinions. He went on to write a book entitled *Personal Influence,* in which he concluded that media content was relatively weak.

Lazarsfeld approached the study of media effects by studying samples from the population of Erie County, Ohio. He chose this location because it best represented the way the United States voted. He specifically examined people's predisposition, their interests, and cross pressures. His study was a cross-sectional study: taking place during one year.

In contrast to Lazarsfeld, McCombs and Shaw believed in the ideas of the "agenda setting position." This entailed a belief that "…the press may not be successful much of the time in telling its readers what to think, but it is stunningly successful in telling its readers what to think about." McCombs and Shaw monitored press coverage and public opinion during the 1968 elections in Chapel Hill, North Carolina. They examined the issues that got the most coverage in the press and whether people ranked those issues in relation. They found that there was a close correspondence between what was in the news and what was on people's minds. This too was a vertical study, like Lazarsfeld's.

Iyengar and Kinder took a different approach in there study. They took the agenda setting approach and applied it in a longitudinal study. They believed that it is necessary to collect data over a longer period of time to control for the real world conditions. They tracked energy, inflation, and unemployment on a month by month basis from 1974 to 1980. Additionally they examined the public's opinion. For energy and inflation they found that people's opinions were dependent on presidential speeches and that real world conditions had no effect. For unemployment they found that TV coverage had a minimal effect and that presidential speeches had no effect. Their study supported that media coverage might be more important in terms of influence when its about issues not directly close to people. Unemployment was just more salient than energy and inflation.

Iyengar and Kinder did find evidence of agenda setting in their study. The news stories that were stressed were those that people said were important. As a result of their findings Iyengar and Kinder said that media content affects the way people see the world. That media content had the ability to affect the criteria by which individuals' judge which issues are important.

The findings of "minimal effects" and "agenda setting" researchers were contradictory and complementary. The agenda setting approach does not seem to work on everyone. Some people are simply less affected by what they watch. One good example would be those who are really interested. The minimal effects approach was in question because it was thought that the wrong questions were being asked. Some people believed that they were asking questions that opinion leaders had access to. This would mean that the study did not accurately represent the news that was happening. Although both types had faults, they were very much alike in those faults. Both had problems applying their theories to the population as a whole. Yet the two were also different because the mentioned studies were all done using a cross sectional approach. However, the minimal effects were done using a cross-sectional and longitudinal approach. Both approaches support the general concept that media content sensitizes people. They believe that exposure to media causes people to become more aware of issues that are prevalent in the news. They are very similar in how people receive this information. The minimal effect puts more of an emphasis on people in leadership positions that influence other people's opinions.

The similarity between the minimal and agenda setting approaches also lies in their portrayal of leaders. The minimal effects approach states that a leader influences what people follow and the agenda setting approach also hints at this. In Iyengar and Kinder's study, it is proven that the president greatly influenced people's opinions. However both approaches fail to consider the influence of other people in power when it comes to influencing opinions. Both approaches fail to focus on those people who deliver the news to people. People who watch the news, even on an infrequent basis, could probably tell you who their favorite news reporters are. People build connections with these news anchors and tend to trust what they say. This is especially clear in the case of Tom Brokaw or Peter Jennings. They are people of great admiration.

The effects of media have been approached in a variety of different ways during the past century. It seems that the one tie between the minimal and agenda setting approach is that of leadership. In both instances those people who are seen as leaders have great influence over sensitizing people to see something as being important.

Chapter Five

How Social Movements use the Internet

Political theorists like Alexis de Tocqueville have long recognized the importance of citizen associations for the practice of democracy. Through participation in associations, citizens both receive an education in public affairs and create centers of political power independent of the state (Klein, 1999). Essential to participation in an association is a forum, a communication space that allows many-to-many communication. However, participation in forums suffers from many barriers, such as the need to meet in one place, at a specific time, and the potentially high monetary costs of participation. Online forums on the Internet avoid many of these barriers, and hold the promise of allowing associations to be more responsive, more robust, and better able to unite more members. Increasingly, social movements are using the Internet. The Internet is revolutionizing the way activists organize campaigns because it can reach more people, more rapidly, and more cheaply than other forms of communication.

Alexis de Tocqueville believed the meeting hall and newspaper were the two technologies needed to achieve a communication forum. Each has its advantages and disadvantages though. A meeting hall is a true forum that allows participants to engage in face-to-face communication. It allows opinions to be maintained with a "warmth and energy that written language can never attain" (Tocqueville, 1835). However, a meeting hall requires all participants to assemble in a single location. The synchronization of schedules, the costs of renting the hall, and traveling to the location also are barriers. Newspapers provide a solution to some of the meeting hall's barriers because they are dispersed to members "every day without having met" (Tocqueville, 1835). A newspaper can unite members in daily communication, maintaining the unity needed for effective citizen action. They are low cost, overcome geographical barriers, and attract citizens to an issue or common interest. However, a newspaper is not a true forum; it allows only for one-to-many communication, rather than many-to-many communication.

Culture is the way people in societies live their lives, as well as the artifacts—songs, dances, pictures, stories—they produce that express or celebrate those lives. Culture has endless potential for those interested in social movements, social change, and social being. Looking at culture in the broad sense reveals the way in which people insist on making various worlds out of the one into which they were born. There is much to be learned from the way different groups of people use elements for resistance, change, and revolution (Austin-Smith, 1996).

From the rainforests of the Mexican state of Chiapas, to the streets of small town U.S.A., to the capitals of Europe, the Internet is one of the hottest tools in the burgeoning arsenal of protest. Yet the tale of Internet-inspired diffusion is a cautionary one, without a predictable end.

An understanding of the role played by the Internet in the rapid diffusion of protest should begin with a view of changes taking place in both the study and the practice of contentious politics. Social movements, on one hand, are sustained interactions between those with power and those without it. Typically, movements and their participants are outsiders, lacking in adequate formal representation and remaining outside established political institutions. Movements also tend to rely frequently, but not exclusively, on non-institutional tactics, creating disruption to promote social and political change or making claims on the state. Thus, while movements are often linked to political institutions, allying with traditional political actors and relying on more mundane lobbying tactics, social movements also clearly differ from conventional political action.

The Internet has changed the way diffusion works. While many definitions have been offered, the following simple version by Michaelson (quoted in Giugni 1998, 95) works well: diffusion is "the process by which an innovation (any new idea, activity or technology) spreads through the population."

The Internet challenges the dynamics of diffusion in ways beyond those encouraged by the so-called CNN effect of television. First, the diffusion of ideas and tactics occurs between individuals and groups much more quickly, potentially reducing the relevance of cultural connections or interpersonal networks for the spread of contention. Second, the process of Internet-carried contention, going against authority, may be less contained or constrained by activist-led movements but, rather, unleashed into a type of global electronic riot. In fact, it might be worth asking whether the Internet is encouraging new styles of collective action quite different from the styles attributed to social movements over the past twenty-five years, and if so, whether this postmodern phenomenon of cyber-diffusion portends a reawakening of those favored objects of study of the collective behavior school, including riots, fads, and panics (Johnston and Lio 1998).

The Internet is far from routine in its impact on contentious strategies, as it offers a diverse menu of options to those seeking new channels for protest. Organizational Web sites present a variety of options, including posting messages on a discussion board, joining a listserv to receive up-to-date information on a campaign or new event through an e-mail account, sending e-mail to politicians, government agencies, or other activists, and searching on related links for additional information related to various campaigns. This last option is an important facet of a Web site, as such sites serve as information clearinghouses for vast amounts of material relevant to protest.

With this collection of resources, the Internet removes barriers to the rapid diffusion of protest ideas, tactics, and strategies. First, the speed by which information can be disseminated affects the global diffusion of protest dramatically. When a message is posted on a Web site, it is immediately accessible, crossing time and geographic boundaries without a concern for time zones, media coverage, or customs barriers. As Maude Barlow, an activist involved in the campaign against the Multilateral Agreement on Investment (MIA), noted in 1998, "If a negotiator says something to someone over a glass of wine, we'll have it on the Internet within an hour, all over the world." This comment by the head of the 100,000-person-strong Council of Canadians (COC), a public interest group that mobilized via the Internet against the MAI, suggests how strategic a tool the Internet has become for actors engaged in contention. The Globalization and MAI Information Web site, managed by volunteers in Vancouver, British Columbia, for example, has compiled an international smorgasbord of hyperlinks to individual campaigns around the world, immediately accessible to groups and individuals to peruse at the click of a computer keyboard (Ayres, 1999).

Similarly, the Internet has significantly reduced those barriers of place that certainly slowed if not hindered the spread of information. Through the process of cyber-diffusion, groups as remote as Zapatista rebels in the Mexican state of Chiapas can attract a global audience to their cause, encouraging supportive protest in New York City without ever leaving the rainforest (Schulz 1998). Whereas protest frequently centered in urban areas—taking to the streets and attending to the barricades in the style of the contentious French (Tilly 1986)—today, a committed, Internet-connected activist can attend to the "virtual barricades" from a bedside table on a small island in the South Pacific. This should not be taken as a sign that the street protests of old are being replaced by Internet protest. The recent and rapid spread of Kurdish protest across Europe and North America, for example, suggests otherwise. But Internet-inspired protest simply diffuses much more quickly and efficiently across geographic boundaries, and, at a minimum, complements street protest (Ayres 1999).

The ability of the Internet to quickly and effectively disseminate information across borders also bolsters its potential as a medium for empowerment. While some evidence paints a picture of Internet users as lonely, atomized individuals, sinking deeper into depression while lost in a maze of chat rooms (Kraut et al. 1998), other evidence suggests that the Internet does serve as an efficacious tool for those concerned about or committed to a particular cause. Hemophilia activists in

North America have found that the Internet serves as an important tool through which to develop a sense of community and build political activities around the scandal of tainted blood supplies (Kraut et al. 1998). The MAI campaign especially highlighted the Internet's potential for enhancing efficacy across borders-those Canadians who logged onto the MAI-Not Web site received encouragement from New Zealand activists via daily e-mail in support of the MAI campaign. "New Zealanders are talking about the tremendous fight Canadians are putting up against the MAI every day ... each day! Switch on my email and there you are, carrying on the flag of freedom and democracy, and we're encouraged all over again to keep going. Here's smiling at you Canada" (Ayres 1999). The evidence is anecdotal, to be sure, but it is enough to suggest that this "easy riding on the Internet" has provided individuals and groups with a greater capacity to contribute to a contentious campaign (Ayres 1999).

The recent global protests against the MAI provide an intriguing example of the Internet's power to diffuse contentious political behavior. This global campaign, culminating in the April 1998 decision by the Organization for Economic Cooperation and Development (OECD) ministers to halt negotiations, capitalized on the Internet's speed, disregard for geographic boundaries, efficacious potential, and ease of public accessibility. To be fair, the MAI battle was certainly not limited to the Internet: a core of committed international activists led a campaign of street demonstrations, letter writing, petition signing, and public teach-ins, which contributed to the widespread public unease over the proposed deal. OECD negotiators, due to the strife between them, also failed to help strengthen the deal's chances of success. Yet, many participants, including supporters and opponents, as well as outside observers, agree that the Internet played a key role in the global diffusion of public opposition to the accord (Kobrin 1998).

The Internet provided an ideal forum for the rapid diffusion of opposition to the MAI. The Washington, D.C.-based group Public Citizen, for example, placed an early rough draft of the treaty on its Web site (www.citizen.org) in February 1997. From that time until the April 1998 breakup of the MAI talks, word of the previously secretly negotiated deal spread like wildfire. Criticisms of the treaty emerged on hundreds of Web sites, discussion boards, and listservs, where daily traffic in MAI e-mail discussions became commonplace. A contingent international opportunity—a transnational structure yet in its infancy—the MAI nonetheless became a common target around which public concerns and uncertainties quickly became focused (Kobrin 1998).

The Globalization and the MAI Information Centre, a website hosted by the National Centre for Sustainability, of Victoria, British Columbia, provides a glimpse of the Internet's central role as anti-MAI information disseminator (http://www.islandnet.com/~ncfs/maisite). An active site for unfolding news on the MAI negotiations and international campaigns in protest, this site welcomes individuals surfing the Internet with an attractively designed interface that is easy to understand and use. Is a person seeking the names and addresses of elected representatives and media contacts across the United States and Canada? Does he or she want information on how to create an "MAI-free zone" in a local community? Is he or she interested in participating in international discussion and feedback regarding the development of a "Citizen's MAI," an interactive process facilitated by the Internet? All these and many more activities are accessible, and a mere click of the mouse away, for a budding activist seeking to participate in the myriad of transnational protests against the MAI.

The anti-MAI activities of the Council of Canadians (COC) provided a case study of how the Internet has changed the strategies of advocacy groups. The COC, already a 10-year veteran of large-scale campaigns against the U.S.-Canada Free Trade Agreement (FTA) and the North American Free Trade Agreement (NAFTA), became a major global clearinghouse for anti-MAI information. Its website contained up-to-date material on the MAI, including discussion papers, press releases, and links to dozens of Web campaigns against the MAI in locations such as the United States, the United Kingdom, and Australia. The COC also provided names and contact information for dozens of Canadian organizations opposed to the MAI, including group e-mail addresses and related Web sites (Kobrin 1998).

The COC's anti-MAI campaign also stands in stark contrast to its campaign against the FTA and NAFTA ten years earlier (Ayres 1997). At that time, prior to the widespread use of the Internet, the COC typically reached the public via the more costly and time-consuming methods of cross-country meetings and large-scale mail campaigns. It collaborated, in particular, on a highly successful, albeit costly and labor-intensive, public education campaign that involved the placement of an anti-FTA comic book in hundreds of thousands of English- and French-language newspapers across Canada. By contrast, during the MAI campaign, information critical of the MAI was immediately disseminated across Canada via the Internet as soon as it was received by the COC. "If we know of something that is sensitive to one government, we get it to our ally in that country instantly," boasted the head of the COC.

Ultimately, the COC was only one of hundreds of organizations across the developed and developing world that fed a steady stream of anti-MAI information onto the Internet for global public consumption. It lifted the curtain of secrecy that had for years shrouded the OECD MAI talks, and it forced negotiators to begin to openly address concerns that had been dramatically amplified on the Internet. The Internet's global reach, its speed, its immediacy, and its public accessibility proved to be deciding factors in pooling the concerns of disparate people from far ends of the earth. One observer noted, "The Internet allows anti-MAI activists to reach large numbers of people at little or no cost, who normally would never hear of an investment treaty negotiated in a far away place and would never think that it might affect them directly" (Kobrin 1998, 107).

It is important to reiterate that the anti-MAI campaign did not begin, nor did it end, with the global chorus of Internet-fed dissent that peaked in the spring of 1998. Well-organized and veteran popular organizations had provided the groundwork for the heightened cyber-contention with months of cross-country and transnational coalition building. In Canada, for example, the MAI Network emerged as a cross-country coalition of social advocacy groups months prior to the springtime flurry of Internet protest, while the MAI Inquiry—public hearings on the impact of the MAI and economic globalization on Canadians—continued into the following fall (Ayres 1999). Yet it seems clear that the Internet provided the glue to bind the opposition that had begun simultaneously in a variety of developed countries. Moreover, the Internet is not replacing traditional methods of protest, but it certainly is bolstering and at times even altering processes of contentious behavior in this technologically interdependent (and dependent) age.

Criticism of the Internet

Rumors are made up of three characteristics: collective behavior, informality, and having the purpose of a constructing meaning (Shibutani 1966). Like other collective actions, rumors are formed and then passed on from person to person, thereby taking on a purpose of their own. This description of rumor could easily be applied to a discussion of the Internet as a communication tool. Like the medium of rumor, as information is passed through certain avenues of the Internet and diffused, it changes. Also, like the Internet, rumors are identified as a means for spreading information in a very casual manner "with a lower degree of formalization procedures, subject matter, and sometimes even the use of gestures" (Shibutani, p.23). Since its inception, the Internet has been discussed, praised, and criticized for its offhand and informal style of communication. E-mail has, in many cases, made the need for formal business writing obsolete. Also, the Web has proved to be a less academic space on which to publish journals and electronic magazines (Fisher, 1998).

The Internet serves as an ideal medium for casual communication. Because of its inherently informal structure, it is impossible both to limit who posts information on the Internet and to validate much of the information. Unlike rumors, which usually take place through word-of-mouth interaction, there are no gestures or vocal inflections on the Internet. Information on the Internet can travel and change even faster than a rumor because of a lack of direct physical contact. The flexibility of the Internet is one of the reasons why organizations have spent a lot of time on developing Internet networks and posting information about themselves on it.

Rumors do not have to be false, but that it is only a matter by which people "caught together in an ambiguous situation attempt to construct a meaningful interpretation of it by pooling their intellectual resources" (Shibutani, p.17). Rumors are a type of collective problem solving that works much like a social movement. Like rumors, social movements sometimes work on the basis of misconceptions, and sometimes their information is completely true.

Examples

There are many examples of the Internet being used by people and organizations to stop what they deem inappropriate government and corporate activities. Some of the most famous Internet actions include demonstrations against Mattel, Snapple, and the U.S. Navy.

The Mattel action in 1992 was in opposition to the Teen Talk Barbie Doll. When women academics heard that the new doll made comments like "math class is tough," they used e-mail to show their opposition (Myers, 1994). In the Snapple case, false information stating that the company supported the Ku Klux Klan flew around the Internet. Two years ago an electronic memorandum revealing an unverified U.S. Navy cover-up of a missile downing TWA flight 800 caused havoc on the Internet (Stevens, 1996). In all of these cases, the informal structure of the Internet helped gain attention for the issue (Fisher, 1998).

Barriers on the Internet

Language: Until recently communicating through e-mail in non-English languages was only possible if the language used Roman characters. Presently, most computer networks support software that enables the use of other scripts, such as Chinese characters. In addition, Netscape has designed a browser that supports English, Japanese, and Chinese scripts therefore working multilingually (Internet Explorer has a similar feature as well).

Technology: The discrepancy between the levels of technological capabilities in different countries. Without effective telephone lines, accessing the Internet is frustrating and sometimes even impossible. Many countries also have other technological limitations: in China and Russia, the infrastructure for very high speed links is almost nonexistent (Computer Science and Telecom. Board).

Access to Institutions and Individuals: There are people who still cannot afford the costs of connecting to the Internet. Although costs in the U.S.A. have plummeted in recent years, outside of the U.S., both individuals and organizations are faced with the problem of the high cost of access (Fisher, 1998)

Politics: The notion that the Internet provides a virtual democracy in which people can say whatever they think, is not a reality. One example of this is China, which limits public access to the Internet. The Chinese government requires that all Internet users register with a governmental agency, thus limiting information about China leaving the country

More Examples

In most cases, the work of Social Movement Organizations on the Internet is from outside the system. They are trying to solve social problems that have been identified by the citizens and overlooked by the government. By communicating collectively in an informal manner, Social Movement Organization use the Internet like a rumoring device.

A.T.M. FEES

After San Francisco voters approved a proposition to ban A.T.M. fees in November, Wells Fargo Bank of America retaliated by cutting off non-customers to their A.T.M.'s. Marc Keyser, head of California's Consumers Action League, called for a protest against Wells Fargo. On the website he advises calling the Wells Fargo 800 number and listening to canned tape on how to use the service for 30 minutes a day for 30 days. Keyser claims it costs Wells Fargo three dollars for every 30 minutes. In hopes of gumming up the company computers, activists can also send educational material "like the encyclopedia or bible" to the corporate e-mail address because, he writes, "these bankers missed something in their education" (Bunn, 1999).

Rampant Capitalism

Decadent Action, a "consumer terrorist" group of people working to undermine the monetary system "at their leisure," organized the fourth World Phone In Sick Day on April 6th, the first day of the new financial year. The group has already had success with its "sick-out" strategy; for the first Sick Day, some 2,000 British Airways employees took part, and the group has been credited with inspiring strikes of British prison guards and Irish police. As the group describes itself, "Decadent Action are the man and woman sitting next to you at the cocktail bar, they have money in their pockets and mischief on their minds" (Bunn, 1999).

Marginalization of Fathers

In mid-June, members of FARCE (Fathers Awareness of Rights and Custody Equality) are planning a weeklong picket on the steps of the Capitol to coincide with the second Congressional Fatherhood Task Force, on June 14. Four days later (on Father's Day), the group has scheduled a march up Constitution Avenue and a celebration including "music and clowns." Topics to be discussed at the protest are: "your right to be a loving father," "your rights as a custodial parent," "dealing with the system" (Bunn, 1999).

World Debt

The site for Jubilee 2000 proclaims "biblical tradition calls for a jubilee year, when slaves are set free and debts canceled." For a host of religious and community groups—including the National Council of Churches of Christ and the United States Catholic Conference. Groups across the country have collaborated electronically to conduct a "rolling fast," which moves daily from organization to organization (Bunn, 1999).

Conclusion

The structural characteristics of the Internet greatly differentiate it from other technologies for creating forums. The Internet is freer from the constraints of time, space, and money. A final impact of the Internet is in increasing citizen responsiveness. In response to a crisis or an opportunity, ad hoc associations can be more easily created, and existing associations more easily reactivated. A call for action can be announced on listservs in order to attract participants, and a forum can be created quickly and at nearly no cost to participants. The Internet also introduces some new barriers including false postings which create rumors and language barriers. The growth of the Internet will continue, and the number of people and organizations with access to the technology will increase.

Chapter Six

Internet and Business an analysis of *Digital Capital*

Medieval alchemists searched without luck for the magical stone that would turn metals into gold. They never found it, but modern man has discovered something even better: the digital economy. We have only just begun to unlock the secret of how to convert our knowledge into wealth on a grand scale. Digital capital describes a new class of assets which presently serve as the foundation of wealth. In economies of the past you could create wealth if you owned land. This was true in an industrial economy, where the key assets were financial capital, the physical plant, and resources. However, all of these are becoming relatively unimportant, including financial capital. In *Digital Capital*, co-authors Don Tapscott, David Ticoll, and Alex Lowy explain how the Internet has changed traditional ways of thinking and doing business: they describe a new platform for competition called business webs.

In the past decade most leading theorists described intellectual capital as having three key elements:

1. Human knowledge and brainpower
2. Structural capital contained in knowledge management systems, organizations, and culture
3. Customer capital contained in the brand market share of a company

The Internet transforms these three forms of intellectual capital to create something fundamentally new. Human capital changes into Internet work, which you can have but not own. For example, when you fill out a product review on Epinions.com you become part of their human capital. Secondly, structural capital transforms into the main form of capital in new business models. This is true in the eBay business model, which is itself a form of capital because it enables the generation of wealth. Thirdly, customer capital becomes relationship capital because it changes everything about marketing. The brand is no longer a promise or image of conventional marketing: it becomes a measure of relationship capital.

Business webs are the mechanism for the accumulation of *Digital Capital*: the knowledge and relationship based currency of the new economy. Business webs can be fluid, highly structured, or amorphous. Most important is an amorphous situation, where sets of contributors come together to create value for customers and wealth for their shareholders. The contributors usually include distributors, commerce services providers, suppliers, infrastructure providers, and customers. However, in most business webs, each participant should focus on a limited set of core competencies: the things it does best.

The common element in the companies *Digital Capital* studied is called the dis-aggregation and re-aggregation of value. All the companies start with a value proposition: something they thought would interest customers. For example, ETrade targeted customers wanting a good broker that would provide access to the market, advice, and the ability to do trades. The company then disaggregated that value proposition into its elements: bringing partners together on the Internet, to deliver the value to customers. However, all the companies didn't fully understand what they had done or how they had gone about doing it.

Business webs are an inevitable new force on the business landscape. The authors predict "that the corporation as we know it is now dissolving because the reason it exists is slowly vanishing." Business webs are replacing the 20th century model of the firm as the universal platform for creating value and wealth in the new economy, and ignoring them would be a mistake for any business.

Overarching Themes to Watch

1. Formulate a successful business web strategy:

- A six-step plan that takes managers from the initial step: dis-aggregating the value proposition that the end-customer receives and experiences.
- Re-aggregating an entirely new set of value offerings in the context of the digital infrastructure.
- Defining the mix of business web types that will improve your competitive advantages.
- Not choosing the one right business web model can be the determining factor separating success from failure.

2. Human Resources changes on the Internet:

- As we move into the world of business webs, the HR profession must reinvent itself.
- Rather than HR management, we need to think in terms of inter-enterprise human resource management, which is human capital in its Internet form.
- Companies must view the employees of their business web's partners as extensions of their own capital.
- Competitiveness and customer value creation depend on accumulating and unleashing digital capital in all its forms. This will require a radical rethinking of tradi-

tional functions like recruiting, conflict resolution, and compensation.

3. Everything about marketing is becoming obsolete:

- Product, Place, Price and Promotion are no longer a valid framework. Old institutions take time to change. But, punishment is proving to be very swift and those that don't reinvent themselves quickly will become obsolete.

- Traditional categories of advertising don't work in cyberspace. In a business web, everyone and everything communicates: multiple ways, all the time.

- Marketing's job becomes focused on accumulating relationship capital. The brand still matters, but as a measure of relationship capital, not as an image.

- To respond to these radical changes, executives need new practices, and fast. The old four P's should be replaced with a new marketing approach called the ABCDEs of marketing: (A) Anyplace, anytime, anyway shopping—replaces place; (B) business web relationships drive revenue; (C) communication works, not promotion; (D) discovery of price replaces fixed price; (E) experience replaces product.

4. Importance of the customer:

- In a business web the customer's role is critical to value creation in all five business web scenarios.

- In the Agoras scenario, customers typically bring goods to market, and engage in price discovery. EBay is the context provider for customers who define the content: the goods that are sold.
- In Value Chain business webs, customers often design and co-service the products. Customers are part of Dell's business web: they are able to configure the product and initiate the manufacturing process.
- In Alliance business webs, customers often create the most value: many Palm Pilot customers create software which they share with others.

5. In the business web outsourcing is nonexistent:

- Managers will no longer view integrated corporation as the starting point for assigning tasks and functions.
- Managers should begin with a customer value proposition and a blank slate for the production and delivery infrastructure.
- Through analysis, businesses will parcel out the elements of value creation and delivery to an optimal collection of business web partners.
- The lead firm in a business web will want to control core elements of its digital capital: customer relationships and intellectual property.

Expanded Theme

Formulate a successful business web strategy:

- Business webs have a great relevance to current technology because; by its definition, business webs are clusters of businesses that come together over the Internet. Each individual company retains its identity; the companies function together, and are able to create more wealth than they could individually.

- Companies like Amazon would be unable to function: the business web includes publishers, customers who write reviews, delivery companies like FED-EX, and thousands of people in its marketing network.

- The new economy is a new business model. Companies are exploiting a new communications medium to change the way they create value for customers. The business web strategy also has a major impact on preexisting companies such as Ford Motor Company. Due to its new business web strategies Ford is achieving new efficiencies in production and in the way it manages inventories, while beginning to provide new, value-added services.

- Many people have been bewildered by the seemingly absurd evaluations for Internet stocks. Using lenses from the old economy, such evaluations are incomprehensible and the capital markets don't make sense. But what many investors know intuitively is that many of these companies are amassing huge digital capital.

- Companies are creating new business models, new networked relationships, and acquiring new networks: all which have given them far-reaching ability to create value and generate wealth. The bottom line is that dot com doomsayers don't understand digital capital.

- These are only the early days of digital capital. Many e-business experiments will stumble and fail, and the markets will react to this. What many analysts and other market watchers fail to understand is that this isn't a "new economy versus old economy" question.

- New business models call for new kinds of digital capital lenses: dot coms can't be evaluated the same way as other companies.

- When the steam engine came along in the nineteenth century, some people wanted to stick with horses because they thought there would always be a need for them. But, others thought the steam engine looked promising, and decided to invest in railroads, in the companies that build locomotives and make products shipped by rail, and in the new communities built in the new territories.

- The real issue is if you are investing in equipment for the horses or in the emerging infrastructure. The Internet is not a product. It's not like biotech from the '80s, as this is not a sector. It's becoming the infrastructure for all sectors that will continue well beyond the next 5 years.

- The wrongfully pessimistic view of the market is supported by The Organization for Economic Co-Operation and Development, which prides itself on education: http://www.oecd.org/. The organization:

"provides governments a setting in which to discuss, develop and perfect economic and social policy. They compare experiences, seek answers to common problems and work to co-ordinate domestic and international policies that…must form a web of even practice across nations."

- OECD also examines whether or not it is appropriate to speak of a "new economy," with the belief that innovation and technology play crucial roles. They support the concept that a range of complementary factors such as the Internet and Internet applications help support the innovation-intensive growth.

- The Economic Strategy Institute (ESI) also supports the concept of business webs and globalization: http://www.econstrat.org/. They believe: "As technology has shrunk time and distance over the past forty years, integration of the world's major markets into one global economy has proceeded at an increasingly rapid pace." And place: "particular emphasis on institutional and structural factors and on the circumstances of the particular industries that make up the overall economy."

- ESI also acknowledges that markets operate with certain boundaries and emphasize a globalization of networks. The members of ESI are visionaries like the authors of *Digital Capital*: they want to share realizations to improve the economy and the way people think.

Considering starting in ecommerce?

From a financial standpoint it seems like a good idea to get involved with e-commerce, considering that industry analysts predict online business transactions will more than triple in the next four years, with revenues growing from $120 billion to $1.3 trillion. However, the tough part for all businesses lies in constructing and maintaining an electronic storefront.

Coming from a family of lawyers, my first suggestion would be to seek advice from an attorney with experience in the field. While this may seem like an expensive proposition at first, it could save the company money and legal hassles in the long-run. This is also important, should you decide to expand the business, sell it, or take it public. Companies must consider exactly how and when they are going to start making money. In addition, before launching the site, an attorney should draft a privacy policy and terms of use guidelines for customers.

The current need for proper legal services is even more important, given the recent incidences of companies illegally selling user information. EBay was recently in the spot light because it decided to alter its privacy policy to allow personal data to be shared in the event of a merger or buyout. Privacy is a very hot issue for consumers, the industry, and Washington. All signs point toward Congressional enactment of comprehensive Internet privacy legislation.

Obviously, building the right foundation for a profitable e-business requires careful consideration and a solid strategy. It's also important to note that a full-service transactional Web site may not be right for your business. If you aren't offering products or services that lend themselves to the Web, or if selling online is not a key objective for your company, consider setting up a brochure-type site instead.

A brochure site simply promotes your business and helps create foot traffic at your office or store. With this site you're not selling products or services online. Instead, customers are provided with basic information, such as your business address, the types of products and services you offer, directions to your offices, and contact information. A good example of this is Joey Reiman's company Brighthouse, which has set up a brochure site at www.brighthouse.com.

Before jumping on the e-commerce bandwagon, here are some things to watch out for:

1. The Internet is always changing:

The technology associated with the Internet moves and changes quickly. This is good for the consumers. However, in order to keep your business relevant it has to be able to change and adapt with the changes in technology. This means that one of the most powerful resources is up-to-date information. Without it, a company will spend valuable time and money on things that are irrelevant. Additionally, avoid long term agreements for services because in a few months these services may be free or cheaper.

2. Always remember your visitors:

The business must be customer oriented. A customer oriented business entails adapting your business for visitors. If you are not offering customers what they want, then the business will not be successful. But this doesn't mean a business should try to persuade its visitors to want what it's offering. Instead, find out what the customers want and give that to them. Ultimately, visitors will make or break the company.

3. Use foundational business principles:

As with other advertisers, Internet advertisements can promise a lot and deliver a little. The Internet is not a get rich quick place anymore. A company will prosper when sound business principles are applied and adjusted to fit a particular niche.

4. Don't rush—lay the proper foundation:

Planning is extremely important in any business. If you want to make money on the Internet you must plan. A plan describes where you are going, how you are going to get there, helps to identify weak spots, and helps to discover how to fix them.

There are several basic steps to complete before transacting business on your Web site. You may consider selecting separate vendors for each step (such as site design, setup, and transaction processing) or you might prefer a vendor that provides an all in one solution, such as IBM's e-business service. Choosing one vendor that offers a suite of e-commerce services can simplify the process and save time and money. As e-commerce has gained popularity, so too has the number of e-commerce packages available. Most of them are suitable for general purposes, but you should take a close look at the software you choose before you commit to it.

Authors Keen and McDonald in *The eProcess Edge* describe four models of sourcing processes: embedded, out-task, in-source, and exceptions. Expanding on his ideas of order fulfillment, the relationship interface, and personalization—all of the following are necessary in an e-commerce environment:

1. Easy product entry/updates:

Most packages allow you to import product information via a spreadsheet. So you don't spend hours re-keying the information. Also, make sure the software allows for instant updating of current products. Systems such as those by Oracle have weekly updates, and Oracle's tech support won't even acknowledge those without the most recent updates.

2. Good photo management:

The number of photos contained on the site will grow as new products/services are added to the site. It's important that the software used for e-commerce makes managing the images trouble-free.

3. Support for associate programs:

Analogous to word of mouth for cash, associate programs allow a company to monetarily reward folks who refer your site to others. But without software support, this feature can be a big headache to administer.

4. Multiple payment methods:

At the very least, the e-commerce system should accept the major credit and debit cards. The best systems also allow you to pay from established accounts, such as Amazon.com's one-click buying. Also automatic authorization is important, unless you're running a low-volume site where manual processing of credit cards is acceptable, you'll want an automatic method so there are no bottlenecks in the order while you verify information.

5. Variations on products:

Make sure the software allows the customer to select the various product options or services, like color, size, and model. Otherwise you'll end up with more pages than you really need. Automatic calculation of shipping and discounts is essential. Surprisingly, many packages only allow you to charge a given price for the product and shipping. You'll be better served with a software package that allows you to discount the cost of the product and the varied amounts for shipping. Many sites allow for coupon codes, such as buy.com and outpost.com. It's also important to be able to charge sales tax for the different states if applicable, which Kozmo.com does for each state it has operations in.

6. International currencies:

If you plan on shipping outside of the United States, make sure the software accommodates the appropriate currency and address information.

7. Security:

You need to make shoppers feel safe sending their credit card information over the Internet. To do so, be sure the software you use supports the industry standard SSL (Secure Socket Layer) protocol. Also, be sure to publicize how secure your shopping software is in several places on the site.

8. Product search:

You want to make sure people looking for your product can find it. Also, back the search with sales support. If someone wants to buy a widget from you, chances are he might also be interested in purchasing a widget AC adapter or maybe even a widget filter. The software should allow you to cross-promote products and suggest add-on products. A brick and mortar example of this would be fast-food restaurants which try and push more items to you: "would you like fries with that."

9. Order tracking:

Once viewers become customers, you'll want to keep them informed. Customers feel more secure when they can track their purchases while in transit. If your software allows this feature, your customers will feel better and you'll decrease the number of calls your customer support staff needs to take. Amazon attempts to do this by not actively listing its customer support number.

Experience shows that an e-commerce strategy that does not stand on sound legal, operational, and customer relations grounds is doomed to failure. Instead, a well-founded systematic strategy that incorporates the different facets of e-commerce is needed. Thus, the question is not whether e-commerce has strategic potential; rather it is how to reach that potential. A practical, systematic, strategic approach following the steps above is needed in order to ensure the effectiveness of the e-commerce effort.

Business processes and success

Business processes determine the nature of a company's capability and involve prioritization and coordination. The growth of the Internet has changed traditional business processes. Before the Internet it used to be that a decision to purchase an application system was supplementary to the business process, or as a way to automate portions of the business process. Often, these systems were "point" solutions that addressed a specific and local need, such as label printing, dissemination of lab test data, or control of a particular process or piece of equipment. As the depth and breadth of the applications that are addressed by systems has expanded, something quite remarkable has happened in the relationship between application systems and the business processes they support: currently there is a merging and blurring between systems and business processes. The change has been so profound that, today, major business process changes cannot be considered apart from supporting systems.

The importance of Information Technology (IT) to the business cannot be underestimated. In fact, systems decisions are becoming more and more one of the most critical decisions that a business makes. *The eProcess Edge* describes that for many years, there has been heightened interest in business process reengineering. With the changing customer and marketplace demands, organizations must continually reevaluate their processes to find better ways of doing business.

At one time, IT's job was to install networks, fix PCs and integrate applications. The role of IT now is to make a company indispensable to its customers. The only way to do that is to insert your company into the business processes of the customers, making your company essential to the execution of those processes. The alternative is to compete on transient factors like price, which is dangerous in the age of the Internet.

When a reengineering effort identifies business process changes, the implementation efforts nearly always involve significant systems changes. In today's working environment, it is usually not an option to introduce manual practices into areas that were previously automated. Users do not tolerate older work practices that increase the time and effort necessary to complete tasks. Tight job markets are increasing the competition for capable employees who do not want most of their energy spent on tedious assignments. It can be detrimental to implementing the process of improvements if employees are fully consumed in manual, time-intensive activities. The best options are those solutions which require system changes to support the new business practices.

For those working in the IT field, this increased importance to the business does not come without additional responsibility. IT personnel must appreciate the impact of a system decision on the business. Systems decisions are understandably made with heavy involvement and influence from those working in IT. Often, IT standards, operating principles, or technical recommendations play a big part in these decisions. There certainly are operating efficiencies and support concerns that come with IT standards. However, standards must be pursued in such a way as to not compromise business effectiveness. A violation of a standard usually has cost and risk implications, and these should be understood and weighed along with all other business impacts.

For those working at the business end, there is a need to increasingly understand the role of systems, and how use of a system can affect the business. Understanding technology, new technical developments, and systems alternatives are now a prerequisite in many business roles. Identifying system changes necessary to support the new practices are essential to implementing business process improvements. Additionally, managing the impact of these changes on the people involved is a critical role.

All of this points to an increasing need for partnership and effective communication between business and IT personnel in the implementation of business processes. The strength of this relationship influences the effectiveness with which business process improvements and the resulting systems work can be implemented. Increasingly, all major systems decisions are strategic. The business practices can simply no longer exist apart from the supporting systems.

In the 1990s, manufacturing companies worked hard to weed out inefficiencies, improve information flow, and foster collaboration within their own organizations by streamlining business processes and deploying ERP systems. In this decade Web-based trading exchanges can provide a platform and opportunity to accomplish many of the same objectives between trading partners in a supply chain. Online exchanges offer a great deal of promise, but significant payoffs still lie in the future.

Still in their infancy, some trading exchanges are only now building connections that facilitate automated transactions.

Others are a step ahead, integrating enterprise-resource-planning (ERP) systems. Time will tell if these and other system-to-system links are completed and the exchanges that survive consolidation begin to provide the value promised by seamless information flow.

The key to exchanges reaching new levels of value lies in the integration of business systems between companies ERP systems, plant systems, financial solutions, and product development platforms. More than just computer technology and translation of data into industry-standard protocols, integration encompasses business process definition, workflow, and event triggers that help manage relationships among buyers and sellers

Another important part of the business process is outsourcing. Companies in today's Internet-driven world must find strategies that work in the new economy. To gain or maintain a competitive edge, companies must take advantage of the best practices of other companies, and the best way to do this is to outsource. Outsourcing has become a dynamic business tool because companies of all sizes and shapes recognize that they can become more profitable and stay on the cutting edge of change by turning over business processes to companies that are more expert in those areas. Leverage is the key to successful outsourcing. One example of the use of leverage is the Application Service Provider (ASP), a fast-growing area of outsourcing. An ASP makes a sizable capital investment in state-of-the-art hardware and first-tier software. Companies that could never afford such options on their own can enjoy the benefits of having them by outsourcing to an ASP.

In bad business processes a company fails to utilize its scale. The use of economy of scale is a powerful concept; if a supplier's process has under-utilized equipment or facilities, it can use computer automation or employ another source of scale. There is opportunity for a supplier to develop alliances with buyers and to build economies of scale in a business process when the underlying technology is stable and there is standardization in the business process. Failure to recognize economies of scale could impair the relationship between a business and its customers.

Faced with new dimensions of competition, organizations only have time to focus on what they do best. Most companies can't afford the time or financial resources to concentrate on every function or process necessary to run their businesses. Yet, low-cost operations and operational excellence in all facets of the company are essential. By divesting themselves of their non-core processes through outsourcing, organizations can improve the level of service, cut costs, and free up time and capital to concentrate on what is most important: how they differentiate themselves from their competitors.

Applying business models to Internet companies

According to Rappa's index of business models (http://ecommerce.ncsu.edu/topics/models/models.html) the Internet changes traditional business models, but there is little evidence of exactly how it does. E-commerce creates an opportunity for different types of new business models, some of which incorporate free services and others that provide goods and services. Wachovia is the nation's fourth largest financial company. Wachovia's website is a good example of the application of new business models (www.wachovia.com).

A financial institution, according to Rappa, would fall under the Infomediary category because the site most likely uses data about consumers and their habits to better deliver the bank's products and services, in addition to providing the consumer useful information. Consumer's who are already members of the bank must register to use some services while others are available to the general public (i.e. applying for credit cards and loans).

The true impact of the Internet on business operations can be seen in financial institutions. As compared to other companies, financial institutions seem most likely to adopt e-commerce as a distribution channel with an emphasis on improving efficiencies. Additionally, banks use the Internet to build relationships. Successful banks use their sites to gather information about the customer that could drive future sales. For example, a small business customer needs certain types of cash management services.

Wachovia's site was also designed in such a way as to offer customers an incentive for use, such as giving customers real time access to their account information. An approach like this is more appealing than, the bank saying that it is phasing out the old way of doing business. So, relationship selling is partially about knowing enough to have services that are continually relevant to that customer. A customer that you have a relationship with becomes a customer with specific needs. Those needs shape how the bank structures offerings. Additionally, knowledge about needs also lets a company sell more than product; it lets it sell valuable information to the customer.

With e-commerce, a bank's website serves as a channel where it could resource accounts to customers by cost-effectively accumulating individual transactions and selling them as an asset. It's similar to what happens with credit cards: a merchant bank processes credit cards, and they are, in effect, absorbing account risk for that merchant.

The value network also serves an important role for a bank. It could involve extending the traditional intermediary role so the bank could actually go into the business of processing accounts receivable for small businesses. In another scenario the bank could offer a fraud detection service for users of EBay, for example. Additionally, a bank could provide a virtual workplace to simplify all processes. The Internet allows a bank to be creative.

Online banks can also incorporate texture and touch as a marketing concept. The texture refers to how rich or distinctive the contact is, and the touch refers to the degree of interaction between parties. For example, if a bank publishes CD rates online, it is a low-touch, low-texture activity. However context-based marketing would use high texture and high touch because it is similar to making an offer based on some change in the customer's life.

Developing relationships is important in bank marketing, but few banks seem to be succeeding at it. This is seen in most banks' strategies: they don't have a service strategy that fully leverages all the information they have about a customer. However, the ones that do, like Wachovia, are experiencing great success. There are others, though, that tend to overestimate their hold or stickiness on the customer, which isn't a good idea.

Banks can also use the Internet to attract potential employees, such as me! It appears that banks with a strong brand name and strong geographical presence would find their website more effective than other web-based job sites. This is because applicants directly interested in the bank would provide a better source of experienced applicants and have relevant skills. However, banks without a strong brand name and geographical presence would most likely prefer web-based job sites because they did not have enough traffic at their website. Wachovia has a strong brand name and presence, all of which will help the bank's success in the future.

The main threat to traditional brick and mortar banks web sites is the growing trend of banks that are only Internet based. As a consumer, I am most interested in the types of online services the bank offers. Some of these also include: interest on checking account balances, free check writing, and low-cost electronic bill payments. Further, does it provide real-time account updates and e-mail alerts on low balances? Or does it offer more robust services, such as the ability to link business accounts with personal accounts? Or can I interface online transactions with PC-based financial management software such as Intuit's Quicken? Questions such as these are essential to the growth of a banks online business and to develop a loyal user base.

A quick check at the GartnerGroup's website unveiled that virtual banks had only about 20,000 customers as of April last year. Further, the largest brick-and-mortar banks have only a couple of million Internet users. To increase users, banks are going to have to make their sites customer friendly because many consumers believe the process is complicated and are also worried about security.

However, in order for banks to maintain an Internet presence they'll probably need to increase fee revenue from services like online bill payments and profit from the cross promotional selling of credit cards, home and car loans, certificates of deposit, insurance, and stock trading. Banks will also save on operating costs by reducing the inefficiencies of paper transactions, monthly statements, credit card statements, and bills.

Chapter Seven

High Definition Television

Television, the most pervasive communications medium of all time, was not invented by one person. Its development was the result of the collaborative scientific process and the entrepreneurial spirit. Now, through another collaborative and entrepreneurial effort, what has become the most widely accepted means of dissemination of information and entertainment is facing, for the first time since the introduction of color, a most revolutionary improvement that promises several breathtaking changes in the way people will receive a major portion of their information and entertainment.

This major breakthrough is described by various names such as advanced TV (ATV) or extended-definition TV (EDTV) but the most widely used term is high-definition television or HDTV. While it is true that HDTV will constitute a significant increase in the technical quality of home viewing, the real questions surrounding its

development bring into play several factors and collaborative elements that have far-reaching implications for the industry and television viewers. The real factors in the HDTV arena involve the economic opportunities for manufactures and broadcasters, obstacles to implementation, and offerings for the consumer.

Explanation

Digital TV (DTV) is the umbrella term used to describe the new digital television systems adopted by the FCC in 1996. As of now, there are two digital TV systems, High Definition TV (HDTV) and Standard Definition TV (SDTV). HDTV defines certain minimum performance attributes that deliver approximately twice the resolution of current TV. SDTV refers to a system that provides a display resolution lower than that of HDTV. Digital television (DTV) technology arose out of the consumer's desire for enhanced audio and visual entertainment. Many satellite systems, as well as DVD disks, use a digital encoding scheme that provides a much clearer picture. In these systems, the digital information must be converted to analog format in order to display it on analog TV, under a standard called NTSC. The image looks great compared to a VHS tape, but it would be twice as good if the conversion to analog didn't happen. There is now a big push underway to convert all TV sets from analog to digital so that digital signals drive TV sets directly. The new digital TV is, basically a computer monitor. It accepts pure digital signals and provides a high-resolution picture that is extremely crisp and stable (Yoshida).

Digital Television (DTV) functions through the transmission of pure digital television signals that are displayed on a digital TV set through a decoder box. The digital signals can be broadcasted over the air, or transmitted by a cable or satellite system to your home. HDTV requires new production and transmission equipment at the broadcast stations as well as new equipment for reception by the consumer.

TV sets in the U.S., Japan, and several other countries use a system that is based on the scanning of 525 lines of information per screen frame. European countries and several others use 625 lines. The various proposed types of HDTV will use 1050, 1125, or 1250 scanning lines, thereby effectively doubling the definition of today's television. Additionally the image will be wider: the standard television system utilized in the U.S has an aspect ratio (screen width to screen height ratio) of 12:9 or 4:3. HDTV promises aspect ratios from 14:9 to 16:9, thereby allowing for an image that is approximately 20 percent wider. This mimicking of the existing film aspect ratio should hold high appeal for today's massive TV viewing audiences (Robin).

In addition to increased resolution and a wider aspect ratio, other technical changes will also be implemented with the adoption of HDTV. Gamma, the ability to accurately capture and reproduce images brightness, will also be improved. Colorimetry, the range of color reproduction, will likewise be enhanced: there will be an approximate tenfold increase in color information compared to the U.S.'s current NTSC system. Finally, luminance, the portion of the TV signal which delineates brightness detail, will be significantly increased (Robin).

Compression will be an essential component in the functioning of DTV systems. HDTV employs a compression and encoding scheme known as MPEG-2, which is already the industry standard for DVD videos and some of the satellite TV broadcast systems. It is capable of delivering stunning images in a reasonable amount of bandwidth. In each image, the MPEG-2 software only records changes to the image and leaves the rest of the image as it was in the previous frame, thereby reducing the amount of data by about 55 to 1. The use of MPEG-2 permits a HDTV receiver to interact with computer multimedia applications directly. For example, a HDTV show could be recorded on a multimedia computer, and CD-ROM applications could be played on HDTV systems. A Digital TV must decode the MPEG-2 signal and then displays it just as a computer monitor does, giving it high resolution and stability. This combination of enhanced visual and aural characteristics will certainly have a positive effect on tomorrow's TV viewer (Yoshida).

Bandwidth limitations

As of now, the greatest number of MHz a conventional wireless TV transmission channel allocates is 6. Current analog systems (NTSC) require a minimum bandwidth of 3.35 MHz to transmit video information without any compression. Attempting to change the current NTSC images to HDTV images creates problems. Composed of 1050 lines and 600 pixels, HDTV needs a bandwidth of 18 MHz in order to transmit. However, since the maximum MHz is one third of the requirement for HDTV, bandwidth limitations not only exist, but in order for HDTV to be spread throughout the world, changes to these limitations must be met (Booth).

Three options are under consideration for how HDTV can exist outside conventional channels of terrestrial broadcasting. The first suggestion was to change the channel allocation system from 6 MHz to 20 MHz, thereby allocating additional space for transmission. Another option was to compress the signal of HDTV to fit inside the existing 6 MHz bandwidths. Since the current NTSC service will not be compatible with these two options, they are not considered to be the primary solutions. However, the last option involves allocating a fixed number of channels for the HDTV signal: with two compressed channels and three uncompressed, the signal's first 6 MHz would be used for the NTSC service, while the rest of the signal is used to support HDTV, providing a good solution to

the bandwidth limitations. Problems which will only be reme-
died through time will still exist with the bandwidth required
for HDTV transmission because of the large volume needed
(Baker).

History

HDTV was pioneered by the Japan Broadcasting
Corporation (NHK) in 1969. NHK's original research and
development goal was to devise a television system whose display approximated that of human vision. Although this quest
was certainly a noble undertaking, NHK and a number of
other HDTV researchers eventually scaled down their aspira-
tions to the more humble task of approximating the resolution
and scope of theatrical 35mm film on home video receivers.
Future HDTV standards may, once again, attempt to dupli-
cate the range of human vision, but this ultimate goal will
more than likely have to be realized through a series of smaller intermediate steps such as HDTV (Harbert).

By 1972, NHK had submitted a draft proposal on its
HDTV system to the International Radio Consultative
Committee (CCIR) which is a worldwide standards-setting
organization and part of the International
Telecommunications Union (ITU). That same year, NHK
introduced the first HDTV system. In 1974, the CCIR established its own committee to study developments in HDTV
and in 1979 NHK actually delivered and tested the first
HDTV system (Harbert).

While the Japanese were conducting these tests, their American and British counterparts were also studying the potentials of HDTV. The Society of Motion Picture and Television Engineers (SMPTE) formed their first HDTV study group in 1977. The first test of HDTV in America occurred at an SMPTE conference in 1981 and was followed by a demonstration in Washington, D.C. The same year, CBS requested permission from the FCC for allocation of the 12 GHz broadcast spectrum for HDTV and began to conduct broadcast experiments in the 12 GHZ spectrum (Harbert).

In 1983, the CCIR began development of a single world-wide standard for the studio production of HDTV material. Prior to HDTV, the only universal format for high quality moving images had been 35mm film. When the standard for high-definition television was finally set in 1996, broadcast and consumer electronics officials predicted that U.S. con-sumers would rapidly adopt HDTV, but it hasn't happened for several reasons. Firstly, there is a loophole in the digital TV regulations. When the U.S. Federal Communications Commission adopted regulations for the roll-out of digital TV in 1997, it required broadcasters to transmit only one digital channel. It did not specify that this be a high-definition chan-nel, which would take up most of the spectrum granted. That meant broadcasters could fulfill the requirement by transmit-ting one digital channel, and use the remaining 80% of the spectrum allotment for other services like data-casting (Ranada).

Another obstacle to rapid adoption is the disagreements between the manufactures and broadcasters. U.S. TV set manufacturers continue to blame the broadcast industry for not producing enough HDTV programming. The broadcasters, in turn, complain that they can't be expected to produce the expensive HDTV programming until more consumers buy TV sets or set-top boxes that can receive it.

Nevertheless, the Consumer Electronics Association predicts that HDTV sets will reach 30 percent market penetration by 2006. Beyond 2006, the year all TV stations have been mandated by the FCC to move from analog to digital broadcasting-HDTV, penetration should increase more rapidly. The change to digital TV entails a change in production methods and, as a result, stations and production facilities around the country are slowly beginning to invest in technologies that will enhance their broadcasts.

Economic Implications

According to the American Electronics Association (AEA), the projection of sales for HDTV sets will total $540 billion a year worldwide by 2010, with $11 billion spent in the U.S. alone. HDTV will spark a transformation of the world television industry. Not only will it cause the creation of an electronic cinema, thereby also transforming the world's film industry and possibly the world's entertainment industry, but it also may affect the advertising industry by altering the way its billions of dollars are spent.

Obviously, HDTV will have profound effects on the world's electronics industry, in general. However, the question of standards will play a significant role in HDTV's effect on the world consumer electronics industry. Since Japan now controls this market, it is understandable that Europe and the U.S. would want to develop their own standards for HDTV and thereby establish or control their own manufacturing and consumer product distribution. This is evident by Europe's Eureka Project, which has developed a different HDTV standard than that of the U.S. or Japan. If two or three different HDTV standards emerge, it will be because of political and commercial reasons as much as technical reasons. Apparently, since HDTV production or transmission standards are generally not patentable, we will experience an "anything goes" commercial consumer market that eventually will translate into trillions of dollars of revenues over the next few decades (West).

HDTV will have a positive effect on the semiconductor, computer, and telecommunications industries on a worldwide basis. Japan's dominance in consumer electronics drives its semiconductor industry. The advent of HDTV set manufacturing will require even more semiconductor chips and some of these chips will be more advanced than those found in today's computers. Consequently, HDTV may very well replace the computer as the predominant force behind the semiconductor industry. As a result, HDTV could, in effect, bring a computer-like device with extraordinary capabilities into every television household worldwide. These sets could function as computers when not in use as TV's. With this in mind, the concept of global village appears to take on yet another new meaning (Bursky).

Since the U.S. currently lags behind both Europe and Japan in terms of HDTV implementation, there might be serious ramifications for portions of the U.S. economy due to HDTV development or the lack of it. The AEA's Advanced Television Task Force predicts that a major share of the future HDTV market is mandatory for U.S. chipmakers or the consequences will be disastrous in terms of maintaining U.S. dominance in the worldwide computer market (Ristelhueber).

The U.S. Commerce Department, aware of this serious threat, has established a consortium of 17 U.S. corporations whose collective goals include HDTV research, development and marketing. These companies include IBM, Apple Computer, AT&T, Hewlett-Packard, Zenith, and Motorola. The Commerce Department will seek exemption from current antitrust laws so that these companies can effectively meet the threat of Japanese or European domination of the HDTV hardware market. The rationale for this somewhat radical approach is that losing the HDTV market could mean the initiation of an ever-increasing attack on other U.S. high-tech industries. Also, the Pentagon's Defense Advanced Research Projects Agency (DARPA) has offered $30 million in grant funds for development of HDTV and related display research (Electronic News).

Current Offerings and the Consumer

Today's TV purchasers face a confusing situation. They want to buy a big screen TV or flat panel set that they can finally afford, but in the background looms the uncertainty of impending obsolescence if they don't go digital. To add to their frustrations, implementing DTV has turned out to be a big challenge for TV designers and manufacturers. Manufacturers have had to wait while standards were solidified, and there is a lot of new technology involved, making it impossible for them to deliver established, and cost-reduced solutions to market. This makes digital television's price point prohibitive for most consumers and is stalling the widespread consumer acceptance of the technology (Bloomfield).

With the FCC mandate that the major markets begin transmitting DTV, more than 100 cities are now on the air. Unfortunately, the number of sets capable of viewing these broadcasts is miniscule, compared to the over-250 million analog sets in use and 20 million new sets sold each year. To date, most of the HDTV's sold are quite expensive: on average over $4,000. These televisions are focused on the high-definition end of the DTV spectrum that requires a dramatically more expensive display than is found in most living rooms today. As a result, there is a demand for an alternative to what consumers perceive as an exclusive club where the price of entry is too high (Larson).

Another factor hindering the HDTV market is that daily, exciting digital broadcast content is mainly still on the horizon, as many broadcasters are simply taking their NTSC content and repeating it on their DTV channels. Digitally produced content is dramatically better than what is broadcast over analog TV today, but most consumers aren't getting to view any of it due to the expensive television sets needed to view the signals (Larson).

However, consumer electronics manufacturers are excited about the potential of DTV. After being accused of stalling the rollout of affordable digital receivers, manufacturers are making a real effort to educate prospective DTV customers with in-store information and network TV advertising. Initial product offerings from consumer electronics manufacturers for digital television in 1998 were big (40 to 60 inches), clumsy rear-projection boxes, employing the 16:9 aspect ratio that did little to generate consumer interest. The latest generation of sets, somewhat smaller in size and less costly, strives to change that. Also on the market are a wide range of PC-based TV tuner cards that are capable of displaying full HDTV resolutions on appropriate multiscan monitors. Indeed, multiscan monitors with TV tuners are being made even larger to accommodate progressive scan signals on sets that look like traditional TVs.

Digital TVs now available generally fall into three main categories: integrated high definition sets that include a digital receiver and display; digital set-top boxes designed to work with current analog sets; and DTV-capable displays that, with the addition of a digital set-top box, offer a complete DTV system. The market is also starting to see a new generation of direct-view CRT displays, from 27 to 40 inches and LCD-based monitors that provide incredible pictures and Dolby Digital surround sound at a slightly reduced cost. There are even digital sets in the 4:3 aspect ratio at a much more affordable price. Since price is an issue with consumers, the economies of scale which have helped cut the cost of other consumer electronics devices will certainly apply to digital receivers as well.

Strategies for DTV receiver placement in home theaters have seen companies offering a large-screen "digital ready" display and making available, at extra cost, a separate set-top box that decodes analog signals and displays them as digital. Additionally, audio has been offered via Dolby Pro Logic surround. The strategy is that these upscale consumers can watch big, beautiful analog pictures now, and later, when more programming becomes available, they can purchase a decoder box to watch digital signals at HDTV resolutions.

These decoder boxes will also prolong the life of current analog sets, as consumers will be able to buy and watch digital programming in analog on their NTSC sets. The benefit of these boxes, besides addressing the legacy issue, is that they can also be outfitted with internal hard drives and special software, from companies like Microsoft, Replay TV, TiVo, and others, which enable a wide range of interactive capability, virtual VCR-like features, and personal TV services. Since the set-top is connected to the Internet, this software can be upgraded, thereby eliminating obsolescence.

The market is also beginning to see a new generation of DTV sets that feature built-in decoders that receive all ATSC formats and display them as a 1080-line, interlaced signal.

Direct Broadcast Satellite (DBS) provider DirecTV has also made arrangements with manufacturers so that consumers will have instant access to DBS services, including HDTV channels, interactive games, Internet access and E-commerce services. Additionally, several companies are offering flat-screen plasma displays that the average consumer may interpret as having a digital receiver, although these beautiful-looking models are currently analog receivers. Some companies have developed digital, 720-line, progressive-scan flat screens, but at this point are far too expensive to be considered serious contenders to the more traditional digital sets (Robertson).

Additional advances have been made in the area of DTV set tuners that enable sets to lock onto and receive a specific digital channel. Most notably, a company called Microtune has developed MicroTuner, the world's first single-chip, silicon-based broadband tuner. The company managed to create a single chip that offers an integrated, universal solution for high-speed media delivery over digital cable, satellite and terrestrial transmission. Microchips like these will enable reliable reception on the smallest of devices, such as a watch or miniature Sony Watchman (Bae & Kim).

In the meantime, there's no doubting that when consumers see HDTV, they want it. Consumers anticipate the day when their TV is more than just a TV; it will evolve into the center of a home network that's totally interconnected with the rest of the house. However, consumers also understand the costs involved and probably won't embrace DTV technology until it becomes affordable.

Current Applications

Currently 183 television stations are broadcasting at least some of their programming as digital television. Concurrently all of the major broadcast networks are offering some kind of HDTV programming, though the individual network affiliates determine which of these programs will be broadcast locally in HDTV. Specifically, viewers living in the large TV markets that can pick up a good, strong antenna signal should be able to watch *The Tonight Show* on NBC, *NYPD Blue*, select movies on ABC, and most of CBS's prime-time dramas and sitcoms in HDTV. In addition many TV producers have quietly been filming their shows in HDTV for several years in order to have a syndication library available when HDTV becomes more common (Michaelson).

The lack of popularity for the wide-screen TV format is the main reason cited by network executives as to why they are not broadcasting digital TV. They say that consumers do not want to see the black bars at the top and bottom of the TV screen. However, *ER* and *The Sopranos*, two of the most watched shows on TV, are currently broadcast in letterbox format.

Other recent applications of HDTV include NHK of Japan, which plans to begin broadcasting Seattle Mariners games in digital formats. The company has the cables in place for ten digital cameras inside Seattle's Safeco field to allow Japanese fans to follow along. Major League Baseball is embracing this venture because it believes that its sport is a good match for HDTV; where viewers will be able to see more of the field. Another sports related HDTV project was announced in March of 2001 by Paul Allen formally of Microsoft. He has revealed his intentions to start a regional sports network, called Action Sports Cable Network that will broadcast entirely in HDTV.

The future of HDTV does not rest entirely with television stations and the FCC; there is also the potential of broadcast media over IP. TeraLogic, 3Com, and 2netFX collaborated on a recently released project that enables HDTV content to flow over standard corporate data networks and the Internet. The companies' technology permits streaming HDTV at 20Mbps over broadband IP networks. This development could lead to the possibility of anyone in the world being able to broadcast HDTV content. This could also enable ISP's, cable television companies, and telecommunication carriers to base new services with higher resolution, while increasing quality of service. Additionally, this streaming HDTV could enhance business-to-business video communications, long distance learning for universities and corporations, and Web-based support for customers (Hachman).

There are still several obstacles that stand in the way of full-fledged HDTV use. There is little motivation for broadcasters to install expensive digital broadcasting equipment when few consumers have bought the costly TV sets to watch the digital broadcasts. In addition, over half of Americans get their TV via cable, and cable operators are currently only required to broadcast the local TV channels of the standard, analog type. Cable companies do not want to carry both the HDTV and analog channels because it clogs bandwidth that could be used for profitable pay-per-view channels. However, a few cable operators, such as AOL/ Time Warner, have begun broadcasting some HDTV programming (O'Malley).

For 2001, the issue that is most likely to slow down the spread of digital television appears to be copy protection. The fear of a Napster-like content piracy phenomenon hitting the movie industry with the release of popular movies in HDTV has become an important aspect for the onset of HDTV. Movie executives have been requesting that Congress impose hardware-based controls and limitations on what can be recorded and copied digitally. HDTV will eventually allow broadcast quality master recordings to be in the hands of consumers, but at some cost to the consumer. Most broadcasters currently don't see HDTV as a viable business model, but new revenue opportunities are emerging.

New Revenue Opportunities

Digital broadcasting has made it possible for broadcasters to provide value added services in addition to traditional content. Value added services are an important consideration for any broadcaster moving into the digital era as they provide new ways to differentiate from existing analog services, attract subscribers, advertisers, subsidize the cost of the infrastructure, and generate revenues. These services are composed of one-way and two-way messaging applications (Yoshida).

Messaging applications allow broadcasters to target their messages to individuals and to select market cross sections. One-way messaging applications can be provided to viewers based on the broadcaster's ability to send messages and descriptions to the TV screen. The broadcaster can efficiently target these messages to individuals and to selected market cross sections. Some examples of one-way messaging include:

- Promotional messages, which help broadcasters direct viewers to specific services ("The world cup finals will start in 5 minutes") and help advertisers to promote their products ("The dealer nearest you is at 467 High St."). Messages can be targeted and displayed in the preferred language of the viewer.

- Coupons and vouchers can be delivered via the TV to individual subscribers or groups of subscribers as part of an advertising campaign.

- Alerts and emergency services such as weather or earthquake warnings, which broadcasters are often required by law to provide, can be disseminated.

Two-way messaging applications require minimal interaction with the viewer at home. Viewers are asked to respond to a simple message that appears on screen. The viewer's response can be cached locally and reported to the broadcaster at a later time. This dramatically reduces the cost of the required infrastructure and allows smoother interaction for viewers, since they do not need to remain on-line nor wait for the call to connect. Some examples of two-way messaging include:

- Viewer lotteries can be used by advertisers and content providers who wish to draw viewer attention. The system will randomly pick a number and store it in the subscriber's smart card. Winning viewers can be personally notified on-screen.

- Viewer quizzes can be used to promote channel loyalty or to attract more viewers to a particular TV commercial.

- Interactive ads take advantage of the fact that viewers are more likely to be engaged by short-attention-span interactivity or lazy interactivity. An interactive ad starts very much like a regular commercial. At a certain point, a banner pops up over the video to offer the viewer additional information, delivery of a brochure or even purchase of the advertised product via the familiar remote control.

Conclusion

The development of high definition television is significant because it poses greater challenges than anything the industry has faced in decades. In spite of focusing on questions that relate to the future of HDTV and its implications, HDTV is, in fact, a reality at the present time. While concerns over HDTV are prevalent in the mind of consumers, awareness and interest about the format is very high and continuing to grow. As more programming turns to digital, manufacturers expect awareness to grow even further. The early excitement has been generated by the outstanding picture and sound quality offered by DTV. In addition, set-top boxes are available to enable today's analog sets to receive the digital TV signals and satellite providers are offering a comprehensive menu of programming options in HDTV. This new format will also present a host of new opportunities for manufacturers in the future; with sales of the digital sets themselves as well as related digital products and home theater products that benefit from the high-performance of DTV.

Chapter Eight

Internship at ABC

During the summer of 1999 I interned at a news television station in New York City owned by ABC. My exposure to the television news world allowed me to see the principal's of the critics of the Mass Culture, including those Paul Lazarsfeld described when he critiqued the agenda setting position.

Throughout the first week and the summer, I was also called upon to do several remedial tasks such as getting coffee, the mail, and making photocopies. These tasks didn't bother me much at first because the other experiences made up for them. I spent time getting to know the other people in the station by volunteering my services. This paid off for me on several instances that are worth mentioning. The first came during the second week at Eyewitness News when I befriended the medical reporter Dr. Jay Adlersberg. He asked me to do some research for him on a story about the cholesterol reducing spreads "Benecol" and "Take Control." I conducted research via the Internet and by watching videos. Dr. Jay than invited me out on a shoot where he was going to interview a doctor about the new spreads. During the shoot with Dr. Jay I learned about the concept of "b roll." B roll describes the extra footage that can be used for a variety of purposes. Take for example, a shot of just Dr. Jay's head as he "pretends" to listen to someone talking. During the editing process this shoot can be incorporated into the interview by overlaying the other persons voice. A more common example of this is when you see a shot of people walking on the street or a doctor talking with a patient. Some b roll, as in the later example, can be reused in other stories. ABC keeps an archive of tapes dealing with a variety of topics and additionally has archives of every news show, and most musical recordings.

I enjoyed doing research at ABC, and oftentimes would look for stories outside of work. During slow news days, when producers were searching for stories, I would approach them with my ideas. The first of these ideas came to me by mail. I received information about a new Internet service that offered to do all of your daily chores for you, like waiting in line at the DMV! I thought what I found would make for an interesting story, so I pitched it to one of the producers. He liked my idea, gave it to a reporter, and the result was a five-minute segment about this new service. I was excited that I found a story and was able to contribute.

Another opportunity to contribute a story came when a discussion of fake identification was brought up during one of the daily meetings. ABC was looking to do an undercover story on fake ids, and I mentioned that I had friends who had them. Everyone was interested, and eventually I was ushered to the investigative department that deals with hidden camera reports. I did research for them on where fake ids could be purchased on the Internet, and told them where in Manhattan they could be found. They wanted to take me out on an undercover shoot where I would be wearing a microphone and hidden camera inside a pair of glasses. However, legal issues arose and we were unable to pursue the story in Manhattan. But the legal department was able to find a loophole in New Jersey laws, so we moved the operation to there. Another intern and I entered various shops in New Jersey and attempt-ed to buy fake identification. It was a hot day and we ended it without any takers. The story was postponed because they needed to find new locations. But I had helped to do the ini-tial research and actually got to go undercover.

The third and final highlight of my internship at ABC came during my last week of the internship. They were short of reporters that day and needed someone to go to Yankee Stadium to interview some of the players. I volunteered, and was given a camera crew and a press pass to enter Yankee stadium. Once at the stadium we were immediately allowed in, and we were taken to the locker room along with several other local news stations. I was given the microphone and I got to hold it as Joe Torre and Bernie Williams, spoke. It was amazing to be in the Yankee locker room and to be so close to the players. I was shaking the whole time, I simply could not believe where I was. The footage I got was needed immediately. So after shooting it, we went back to the satellite truck where it was broadcast back to the station. That night I saw the sound bites I recorded on the news, and it was a great feeling to know that I contributed to it.

Through my internship at ABC I saw the importance of the selection of stories and those who deliver them. Stories were selected based on several factors. One factor was the availability of a crew and access to where the story was taking place. This often involved coordinating satellite feeds and with other affiliates. There were only a limited number of reporters at ABC and most were only assigned to one story a day. The biggest limitation on the amount of stories that were covered was the amount of editors present. Each story that was pre-shot had to be edited, and time was allotted between all the editors. I witnessed one occasion where a lead story was still being edited minutes before the newscast was to start. The tape was taking longer to edit, and the story had to be bumped to a later part of the newscast. This is one of the worst things that can happen during a broadcast because the station is competing with other stations. By failing to get an important story in at the beginning, they potentially lost viewers.

Stories were also selected based on the audience that, according to research, watched WABC-TV. The importance of this was made clear when I approached a producer about a story. I had seen information about new technology and the future of cars. I pitched the idea to the producer who immediately dismissed it. I then questioned him for a reason, and he told me that it was something "our audience" wasn't interested in. I was shocked because I thought the station would try to appeal to as many groups as possible.

Another influence on story selection was the time of year. If it was ratings time, more emphasis was placed on covering a wide range of stories. This also put more pressure on the reporters to quickly deliver their stories. Since the newscast was divided up by the second and extra ten seconds on a live shot could be damaging. In order to deliver more stories, reporters were instructed to give short lead-ins to their packages. The atmosphere became tense during ratings because there was a great need to find good stories. During the daily meetings everyone was aware of the need to diversify the stories being covered. During one meeting someone brought up another story involving a death. A few of the producers immediately reacted against the story noting that the top three stories all involved similar cases.

Through researching the history of television I became a critical thinker. I was able to better handle all the new situations that I experienced because I had a sense of their purpose. The internship at ABC was a positive experience. Everyone I encountered was able to provide me with insight into the industry, although sometimes in unpleasant ways. I realize that as an intern I didn't command respect and that most of the work was grunt work. However many of the people acknowledged that they were once in our shoes and treated the interns as they wanted to be treated. I felt a great sense of pride when I returned home each night and sat down to watch the news. By working at a news station I was also more aware of current events. I also became more interested in current events because the more knowledgeable I was, the better able I was to propose new stories.

Conclusion

The challenges facing both the television and Internet are in definition and profit. The rise of the Internet has not forecasted the end of television. But instead, like with radio, television must redefine its place in the home. The television, which was once the centerpiece in the house, is becoming similar to radio. It may soon be "common place for people to move seamlessly from one medium to another on the same delivery platform – TVs or PCs" (Nielsen). Nielsen's research also shows that there is no indication that Internet usage "cannibalizes" television usage. Instead it provides a vehicle to supplement advertising. Television is also creating new ways for profit by reaching out to international markets and through technological advances.

Both the television and Internet industries have redefined their roles because of changes in technology. Internet companies are using the television to pitch their products and services, whereas television companies are wearing two hats, often producing television and Internet content. The television was rapidly integrated into people's lives because it was entertaining. It provided an idealistic setting for advertisers who wanted to reach specific audiences. The Internet still remains secondary to television in terms of amount of people with access.

However, it provides a new ground for advertisers because those on the Internet are more affluent and educated. The Internet still continues to struggle with ways to make money. In this new age of the digital economy a new doorway has been opened to a partnership between television and the Internet that will reshape them as television did to the radio.

About the Author

Eugene Hertzberg is a graduate of Emory University in Atlanta, GA. He graduated with a Bachelor of Arts in Sociology in May 2001. He was born and currently lives in New York City. This is his first book.

References

Austin-Smith, B. (1996) "When we talk about culture." *Canadian Dimension*, 30(4), 44-46.

"American Council on Education." Online. Available: http://www.acenet.edu.

Ayres, Jeffrey. (1997) From National to Popular Sovereignty? The Evolving Globalization of Protest Activity in Canada: *International Journal of Canadian Studies*. 16,107-23.

Baker, Dan. *Electronic Design*: "Measure Uncompressed Serial-Digital HDTV signals with a 2-Ghz Scope." 04/17/2000, 48(8).

Baker, W. and Faulkner, R. (1991). "Role as Resource in the Hollywood Film Industry." *American Journal of Sociology*. Vol. 97, 279-301.

Bae, Seong-Ok; Kim, Seehyun. *IEEE Transactions on Consumer Electronics*: "A Single-Chip HDTV A/V Decoder for Low Cost DTV Receiver." 1999, (45)3.

Bagdikian, Ben. *The Media Monopoly*. Beacon Press, 2000.

Barnes, B. and Thompson, L. M. (1994). *Power to the People (Meter): Audience Measurement Technology and Media Specialization, in Audience Making*. SAGE publications, CA.

Baughman, James *The Republic of Mass Culture*. Johns Hopkins University Press, 1997.

Bloomfield, Larry. *Broadcast Engineering*: "What the set makers have to say." 2000, Vol. 42 Issue 14.

Booth, Stephen. *Adweek — Midwest Edition*: "Mixed Signals." 07/10/2000, Vol. 41 Issue 28.

Bunn, A. (1999) Protester's Delight: *New York Times Magazine*, 149(51741) p. 46.

Bursky, Dave. *Electronic Design*: "Advanced television, multimedia are keys to revitalization." 1999, 47(1).

Carroll, Jim *Internet Handbook*, Prentice Hall Canada 1997.

Computer Science and Telecommunications Board. (1994): *Realizing the information future*. Washington D.C. National Academy Press.

Denke, Conrad. *Broadcast Engineering*: "The future of television." 2000, 42(14).

Deise, Martin V. et al. *Executive's Guide to E-Business : From Tactics to Strategy.* John Wiley & Sons, Inc. 2000.

Electronic News: "Motorola, Sarnoff in HDTV chip drive." 11/10/97, 43(2193).

Fisher, Margolis, & Resnick. (1996). "Breaking Ground on the Virtual Frontier: Surveying Civic Life on the Internet" *The American Sociologist.* 27(1), 11-12.

Fisher, D.R. (1998) "Rumoring theory and the Internet—A framework for analyzing the grass roots." *Social Science Computer Review.* 16(2), 158-168.

Froehling, O. (1997) "The cyberspace 'war of ink and Internet' in Chiapas, Mexico." *Geographical Review.* 87(2), 291-307.

Gamson, W. and Modigliani, A. (1989). "Media Discourse and Public Opinion on Nuclear Power: A Constructionist Approach." *American Journal of Sociology.* 95(1), 1-37.

Giungni, M. (1998) The other side of the coin: explaining crossnational similarities between social movements: *Mobilization.* 3(1), 89-105.

Harbert, Tam. *Electronic Business*: "A disaster by definition." 2000, 26(13).

Hachman, Mark. *Electronic Buyers' News*: "TeraLogic IC targets HDTV." 04/05/99 Issue 1154

"History of the Internet and the World Wide Web." Online. Available: http://wdvl.internet.com

Honan, William. "College Freshmen's Internet Use a way of Life, but Disparities Emerge." *The New York Times*. January 25, 1999.

Iyengar, S. and Kinder, D. *News that Matters*. University of Chicago Press, 1987.

Johnson, Hank, and Shon Lio. (1998) "Collective behavior and social movements in postmodern age: looking backward to look forward." *Sociological Perspectives*, 41(3), 453-472.

Keen, P. and McDonald, M. *The eProcess Edge: Creating Customer Value & Business in the Internet Era*. McGraw-Hill 2000.

Kobrin, Stephen. (1998). "The MAI and the Clash of Globalizations." *Foreign Policy*, 112, 97-109.

Klein, H.K. (1999) "Tocqueville in cyberspace: Using the Internet for citizen associations." *Information Society*, 15(4), 213-220.

Kraut R., Vicki L., Michael P., Sara K., Tridas M., and William S.(1998). "Internet Paradox: A Social Technology That Reduces Social Involvement and Psychological Well-Being?" *American Psychologist*, 53(9),1017-31.

Larson, Megan. *MediaWeek*: "The High Cost of High-Def." 04/17/2000, 10(16).

Lazarsfeld, Paul. Et al. *The Peoples' Choice*. New York, 1944.

Litman, B. and Ahn, H. (1998). *The Motion Picture Mega-Industry.* "Predicting Financial Success of Motion Pictures: The Early 90's Experience." Boston: Allyn and Bacon.

McCombs, Maxwell E. and Donald L. Shaw (1972). "The agenda-setting function of mass media." *Public Opinion Quarterly.* 36(2), 176-187.

Michaelson, Elizabeth. *SHOOT*: "CBS To Stay With HD In Primetime." 2000, 41(35).

Myers, D.J. (1994). "Communication technology and social movements: Contributions of computer networks to activism." *Social Science Computer Review*, 12(2), 250-260.

O'Malley, Chris. *Popular Science*: "HDTV—Ready, Set, No." 2000, 257(6).

"Pew Research Center" Online. Available: http://www.tvrun-down.com.
Ranada, David. *Stereo Review's Sound & Vision:* "Laying Down the Law." 2000, 65(10).

Ristelhueber, Robert. *Electronic Business Today*: "Chip makers eye HDTV bonanza." 1997, 23(7).

Robertson, Jack. *Electronic Buyers' News*: "HDTV picture is still quite fuzzy." 2000, Issue 1224.

Robin, Michael. *Broadcast Engineering*: "Digital standards defined." Feb2001, 43(2).

Schulz, Markus. (1998) "Collective Action Across Borders: Opportunity Structures, Network Capacities, and Communicative Praxis in the Age of
Advanced Globalization." *Sociological Perspectives,* 41(3), 587-616.

Tapscott, Don. et al. *Digital Capital: Harnessing the Power of Business Webs.* Harvard Business School Press, 2000.

Tilly, Charles. *The Contentious French.* New York: Cambridge University Press, 1986.

Tocqueville, A. (1835) *Democracy in America*. New York: Vintage Books. Originally published in 1835.

Van-Slambrouck, P. (1999). "Newest tool for social protest: the Internet." *Christian Science Monitor*, 91(142), 3.

West, Janet. *Electronic Media*: "HD production gets on track in Europe." 2000, 19(42).

Yoshida, Junko. *Electronic Engineering Times*: "Interacting with HDTV." 1994 Issue 782.

Yoshida, Junko. *Electronic Engineering Times*: "HDTV's story: Fits, starts and setbacks." 1996 Issue 903.

<u>Notes</u>

Notes

<u>Notes</u>

Notes

<u>Notes</u>

<u>Notes</u>

<u>Notes</u>